FUN FACT FILE: US HISTORY!

20 FUN FACTS ABOUT US MONUMENTS

By Heather Moore Niver

Gareth Stevens
Publishing

Please visit our website, www.garethstevens.com. For a free color catalog of all our high-quality books, call toll free 1-800-542-2595 or fax 1-877-542-2596.

Library of Congress Cataloging-in-Publication Data

Niver, Heather Moore.
20 fun facts about US monuments / by Heather Moore Niver.
    p. cm. — (Fun fact file: US history!)
Includes index.
ISBN 978-1-4339-9209-4 (pbk.)
ISBN 978-1-4339-9210-0 (6-pack)
ISBN 978-1-4339-9208-7 (library binding)
1. National monuments—United States—Juvenile literature. 2. Historic sites—United States—Juvenile literature. I. Niver, Heather Moore. II. Title.
E159.N58 2014
973—dc23

First Edition

Published in 2014 by
Gareth Stevens Publishing
111 East 14th Street, Suite 349
New York, NY 10003

Copyright © 2014 Gareth Stevens Publishing

Designer: Sarah Liddell
Editor: Greg Roza

Photo credits: Cover, p. 1 Galyna Andrushko/Shutterstock.com; p. 5 Glen Allison/Stockbyte/ Getty Images; p. 6 A L Christensen/Flickr/Getty Images; p. 7 Mark Chivers/Robert Harding World Imagery/Getty Images; p. 8 Allan Baxter/The Image Bank/Getty Images; p. 9 Raymond Boyd/Contributor/Michael Ochs Archives/Getty Images; p. 10 Neta Degany/ Stockbyte/Getty Images; p. 11 Pawel Gaul/Vetta/Getty Images; p. 12 Kent Nishimura/ Stringer/Getty Images News/Getty Images; p. 13 Panoramic Images/Panoramic Images/ Getty Images; p. 14 Mmphotos/Photolibrary/Getty Images; p. 15 photo courtesy of Wikimedia Commons, Little-bighorn-memorial-sculpture-2.jpg; p. 16 photo courtesy of Wikimedia Commons, FortFredMagazine.jpg; p. 17 Richard Cummins/Robert Harding World Imagery/Getty Images; p. 18 Paul D. Slaughter/Photographer's Choice/Getty Images; p. 19 Capitanoseye/Shutterstock.com; p. 20 VisionsofAmerica/Joe Sohm/Photodisc/ Getty Images; p. 21 Kevork Djansezian/Staff/Getty Images News/Getty Images; p. 22 photo courtesy of Wikimedia Commons, Aniakchak-caldera alaska.jpg; p. 23 photo courtesy of Wikimedia Commons, Josie Morris Cabin.jpg; p. 24 Karl Weatherly/Photodisc/ Getty Images; p. 25 Allan Montaine/Lonely Planet Images/Getty Images; p. 26 Gary Koutsoubis/Flickr/Getty Images; p. 27 John Elk/Lonely Planet Images/Getty Images; p. 29 Kevin Moloney/Aurora/Getty Images.

Printed in the United States of America

CPSIA compliance information: Batch #CS13GS: For further information contact Gareth Stevens, New York, New York at 1-800-542-2595.

Contents

Words in the glossary appear in **bold** type the first time they are used in the text.

Protecting People and Places

A US national monument is meant to **protect** an area with at least one major resource. Historic sites, natural areas, or scientifically interesting places can be monuments. This can include the remains of a **prehistoric** Indian settlement, important historic places, or nifty natural spaces.

Congress can name a national monument and so can the president. President Theodore Roosevelt recognized the first national monument in 1906. He chose Devils Tower in Wyoming. The United States has more than 100 national monuments.

Devils Tower National Monument looks really cool, and people like to climb it. The Lakota and other Native American groups also respect it.

5

FACT 1

Hundreds of workers spent 14 years carving Mount Rushmore with chisels, drills, jackhammers, and dynamite.

Between 1927 and 1941, workers **carved** the giant heads of US presidents George Washington, Thomas Jefferson, Theodore Roosevelt, and Abraham Lincoln into a mountain in South Dakota. From chin to top of head, the presidential faces on Mount Rushmore National Monument are 60 feet (18 m) tall.

Mount Rushmore National Monument was made to celebrate the first 150 years of the United States.

The Lincoln Memorial has 36 columns. There were 36 states when Lincoln died in 1865.

FACT 2

If the statue of Abraham Lincoln in the Lincoln Memorial could stand up, he would be 28 feet (8.5 m) tall.

The Lincoln **Memorial** in Potomac Park, Washington, DC, helps us remember our 16th president, Abraham Lincoln. The seated president is 19 feet (5.8 m) tall. Daniel Chester French created the statue using molds made from Lincoln's hands and face.

FACT 3

The Washington Monument is the tallest building in Washington, DC. By law, no other building in the capital city can be taller.

The Washington Monument was built to honor our first president, George Washington. It's a column, or **obelisk**, that's just over 555 feet (169 m) tall. It weighs more than 90,800 tons (82,300 mt). Construction began in 1848, stopped during the Civil War, and continued again in 1876.

The Washington Monument was the tallest structure in the world when it was completed in 1884. In 1889, the Eiffel Tower became the world's tallest structure.

The Jefferson Memorial was modeled on President Jefferson's own home.

The Jefferson Memorial and Jefferson's house, Monticello, were both designed to look like an ancient temple in Rome called the Pantheon. The statue inside is **bronze**, but it was first made of plaster because of a metal shortage during World War II.

The Jefferson Memorial was dedicated on April 13, 1943, which was the 200th anniversary of Jefferson's birth.

FACT 5

In 1886, the Statue of Liberty was shipped from France in 350 pieces. It took US workers 4 months to put the statue together.

The Statue of Liberty's full name is "Liberty Enlightening the World." The statue is over 305 feet (93 m) tall. She stands on Liberty Island in New York Harbor. "Lady Liberty" was a gift to the people of the United States from the people of France.

In 1924, President Calvin Coolidge made the Statue of Liberty a national monument.

This tall Missouri monument was built to allow it to sway up to 18 inches (46 cm) so it could withstand earthquakes and high winds.

FACT 6

The foundations, or bases, of the St. Louis Gateway Arch go down 60 feet (18 m) into the ground.

The St. Louis Gateway **Arch**—built on the banks of the Mississippi River in 1965—represents the US era of westward expansion. This **stainless steel** arch is 630 feet (192 m) tall. It's the tallest man-made monument in the United States.

Rock-and-roll legend Elvis Presley performed a concert to raise money so a US memorial could be built.

The USS *Arizona* Memorial isn't in Arizona, it's in Hawaii. It's named for a US battleship sunk during the Japanese attack on Pearl Harbor on December 7, 1941. The attack killed 1,177 crew members. The memorial was built directly above the sunken ship.

The USS Arizona still holds 500,000 gallons (1.89 million l) of oil. Up to 9 quarts (8.5 l) of oil leak into the sea every day. The National Park Service keeps a close eye on it.

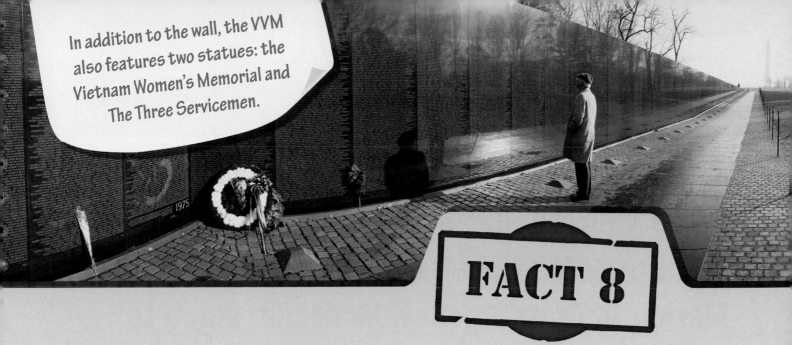

In addition to the wall, the VVM also features two statues: the Vietnam Women's Memorial and The Three Servicemen.

1975

More than 1,400 designs were submitted for the Vietnam Veterans Memorial (VVM). The winning design was by a 21-year-old college student named Maya Lin.

The VVM in Washington, DC, honors US soldiers who served in the Vietnam War (1954–75). It bears the names of 58,272 soldiers who were killed during the war or are still missing. The monument has two sections of wall made from a hard, dark rock called gabbro.

FACT 9

Some visitors and workers at the Little Bighorn Battlefield National Monument Marker in Crow Agency, Montana, claim to have seen ghosts.

The Battle of the Little Bighorn (June 25–26, 1876) was a famous battle between the 7th Cavalry, led by Lieutenant Colonel Custer, and Native Americans led by Lakota warrior Crazy Horse. The Little Bighorn Battlefield National Monument Marker lists the names of the US soldiers who died.

There are 220 US soldiers buried around the base of the monument. However, in 1877, Custer's remains were removed from the site and buried at West Point Cemetery in New York State.

The Peace Through Unity Monument helps tell the Native American side of the story of the Battle of the Little Bighorn.

At least 1,500 Cheyenne, Sioux, and Arapaho warriors fought in the Battle of the Little Bighorn. More than 100 Native Americans died in this battle. The Peace Through **Unity** Monument is a **sculpture** showing life-sized Indian figures speeding across the prairie into battle on horseback.

Although the Little Bighorn Battlefield National Monument Marker was erected just 5 years after the battle, the Indian monument wasn't completed until 2003.

FACT 11

Visitors be warned: there are lots of bugs at Fort Frederica National Monument.

In 1736, James Oglethorpe built Fort Frederica to protect his new colony, Georgia, from the Spanish. In 1742, colonial and Spanish forces fought the Battle of Bloody Marsh. Rumors spread that the river ran red with blood, but only 7 soldiers died.

Fort Frederica has long been known for its icky bugs. Visitors should be prepared to deal with deerflies, chiggers, mosquitoes, ticks, and sand flies!

The Union Army spent the next 4 years trying to win Fort Sumter back from the Confederates.

FACT 12

In the first battle of the Civil War, the Union army of about 80 soldiers lost to the Confederate's army of about 500 soldiers.

Fort Sumter was the site of the first shots of the Civil War.

On April 12, 1861, Union and Confederate forces battled for

34 hours. No one was killed, wounded, missing, or captured.

Today, visitors can reach the fort by boat.

Honoring US Fortresses

Forts on US soil were essential in protecting the British colonies, and then the young United States, from outside forces. The forts shown here were named US monuments because of the historic events in which they played a key role.

Fort Union

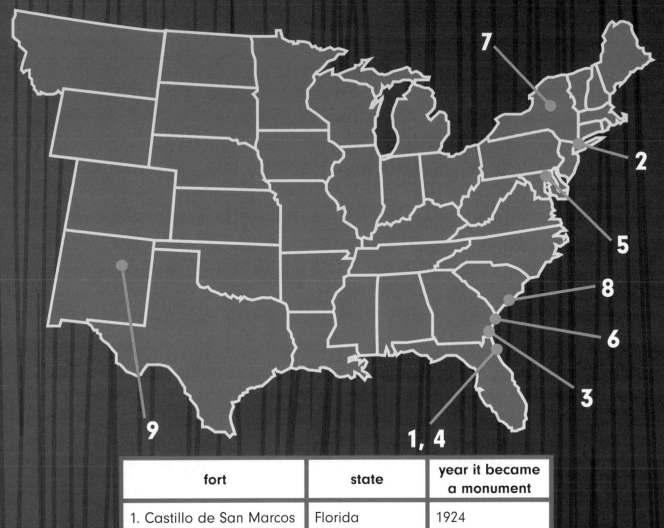

fort	state	year it became a monument
1. Castillo de San Marcos	Florida	1924
2. Castle Clinton	New York	1946
3. Fort Frederica	Georgia	1936
4. Fort Matanzas	Florida	1924
5. Fort McHenry	Maryland	1925
6. Fort Pulaski	Georgia	1924
7. Fort Stanwix	New York	1935
8. Fort Sumter	South Carolina	1948
9. Fort Union	New Mexico	1948

FACT 13

The Wright Brothers National Memorial in Kill Devil Hills, North Carolina, was the largest US monument built for a living person.

The first controlled, powered airplane flight occurred on December 17, 1903. Wilbur and Orville Wright changed the course of history with four successful flights that day. The Wright Brothers National Memorial is a 60-foot (18 m) granite monument constructed on top of Kill Devil Hill. Orville Wright attended the **dedication**.

Before the monument was built, a special kind of grass was planted on Kill Devil Hill—which is made largely of sand—to keep it from wearing away.

¡Sí se puede!

The César Chávez National Monument is still a home and workplace, just as it was during Chávez's life.

César Chávez was a Latino labor leader. He fought for fair working conditions for US farmhands. He always said, "¡Sí se puede!" or "Yes, we can!" On October 8, 2012, President Barack Obama declared the Keene, California, home of César Chávez a national monument.

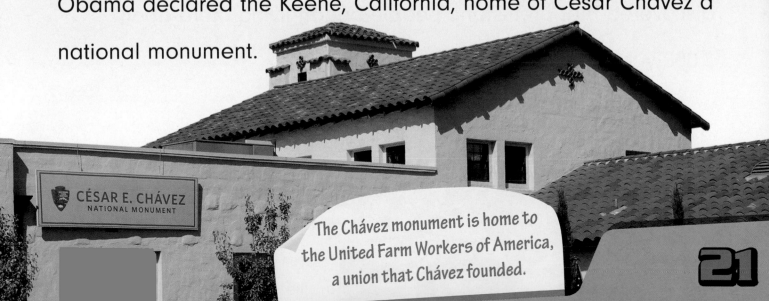

CÉSAR E. CHÁVEZ
NATIONAL MONUMENT

The Chávez monument is home to the United Farm Workers of America, a union that Chávez founded.

FACT 15

About 3,500 years ago, a volcanic eruption in Alaska helped create Aniakchak National Monument.

Aniakchak National Monument and Preserve's most obvious feature is an enormous caldera, or volcanic crater. The caldera is 6 miles (9.7 km) wide and 2,000 feet (610 m) deep. Scientists discovered that prehistoric people began living there about 2,000 years ago.

The weather at Aniakchak is so harsh that it's one of the least-visited national monuments in the country.

FACT 16

Josie Bassett Morris built her own cabin in Dinosaur National Monument and lived there for 50 years without plumbing, electricity, or even neighbors.

Colorado's Dinosaur National Monument protects an area where dinos once roamed. Visitors can see fossils in the rocks. Many years ago, Native American groups lived in this area. They left behind many petroglyphs (carvings on rocks) and pictographs (paintings on rocks).

Scarlet macaws, native to Latin America, were found buried in stone-lined pits under the floors of Tuzigoot National Monument.

Tuzigoot National Monument—south of Flagstaff, Arizona—is an ancient village built by a Native American group called the Sinagua. These buildings were probably built around AD 1000. Between 1933 and 1934, workers uncovered and reconstructed the 110-room pueblo, or village, which includes two- and three-story buildings.

The Sinagua people were farmers, but they had traded with people hundreds of miles away. This explains why scarlet macaws were found in the ruins of Tuzigoot.

American settlers thought the structure was built for the Aztec Emperor Montezuma, but the Sinaguas left their cliff homes 100 years before Montezuma was born.

FACT 18

Montezuma Castle Monument is a 600-year-old, five-story apartment building.

The Sinaguas also built Montezuma Castle in limestone cliffs along Beaver Creek south of Flagstaff, Arizona. The "castle" has 20 rooms. The Sinaguas climbed tall ladders to reach their home. They used water from Beaver Creek to grow corn and beans.

FACT 19

Experts have found more than 50 different colors in the hoodoos, or columns of rock, at Cedar Breaks.

Cedar Breaks National Monument in Utah is a beautiful monument to Earth's history. Years of thunderstorms, snowstorms, and freezing temperatures created an **"amphitheater"** 3 miles (4.8 km) long and 2,000 feet (610 m) deep. The Southern Paiute Native Americans used to live there.

The Paiute called Cedar Breaks "u-map-wich," or "the place where the rocks are sliding down constantly."

In 1924, President Calvin Coolidge called for the Craters of the Moon to be a monument. He said the area was "weird and scenic."

FACT 20

Visitors should watch out for "bombs" at Craters of the Moon in Idaho.

Craters of the Moon National Monument and Preserve is about 750,000 acres (3,035 sq m) of land covered with hardened lava. Volcanoes there erupted eight times between 15,000 and 2,000 years ago. The volcanoes tossed hot lava "bombs," which cooled into shapes called breadcrusts, spindles, and ribbons.

Cool Chimney

In October 2012, President Barack Obama chose Chimney Rock in Colorado as a new national monument. Chimney Rock is both a very cool rock structure and an important place. It was once home to the Pueblo Indians. Chimney Rock has more than 100 **archaeological** sites, which have revealed remains such as bones.

The Forest Service, National Park Service, Bureau of Land Management, and US Fish and Wildlife Service protect and care for monuments. This way, the public can visit and enjoy them for many years.

The rock column in front is Chimney Rock. The other rock column is called Companion Rock.

Glossary

amphitheater: a building with a curved area of rising rows for seating and a main space for events like sports or theater

arch: a structure built in the shape of a curve

archaeological: having to do with the study of the remains of past human life and activities

bronze: a reddish-brown metal that is a mixture of copper and tin

carve: to cut shapes into rock or wood

dedication: a ceremony marking the official completion of a public building or monument

memorial: a place, display, or event that serves as a way to remember a person or event

obelisk: a column of stone with a square base, sides that slope in, and a pyramid on top

prehistoric: having to do with the time before written history

protect: keep safe

sculpture: a work of art made to look like a person or other figure

stainless steel: a mixture of metals that is resistant to rust

unity: agreement or harmony between people or groups

For More Information

Books

Burgan, Michael. *Fort McHenry*. New York, NY: Chelsea Clubhouse, 2010.

Karapetkova, Holly. *The Statue of Liberty*. Vero Beach, FL: Rourke Publishing, 2009.

Schaffer, Julia. *The Washington Monument*. New York, NY: Chelsea Clubhouse, 2010.

Websites

National Monuments
www.blm.gov/wo/st/en/prog/blm_special_areas/NLCS/monuments.html
Learn more about 17 national monuments in 8 western states with pictures, history, and details such as what animals live there.

National Park Service
www.nps.gov
The NPS is a federal agency that manages all national parks and many national monuments.

Index